THE STARTING POINT LIBRARY

MATHS

Circus Maths

THE DANBURY PRESS
A Division of Grolier Enterprises, Inc.

The circus is coming.
Here is the parade.

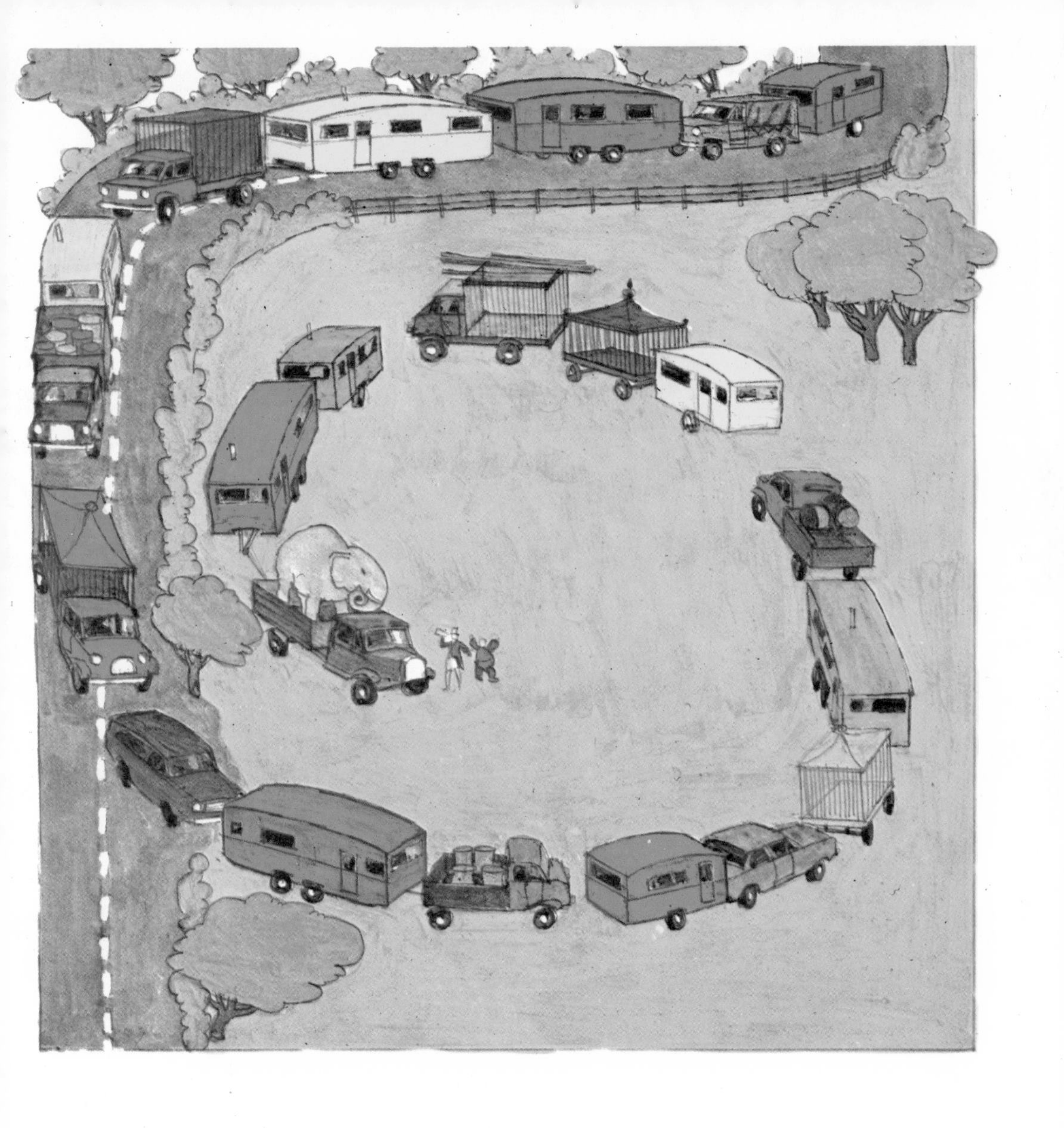

Here are the circus caravans.
How many red ones are there?
Count the long caravans.
How many caravans are long and red?

The men put up the big top.
How do they lift the tent?
What is the elephant doing?
How do the men move the oil drums?

The people go to the circus.
How much must children pay?
What time does it start?
How long does the show last?

The show is beginning.
Find the tallest man.
Where is the strong man?
Is he taller than the clowns?

The ponies trot round the ring.
There are two white ponies.
How many brown ponies are there?
Are any ponies not brown or white?

Here are some balancing acts.
What is the seal doing?
How many children balance the bear?

The clown is painting his face.
One side of his face is like the other.
This is called symmetry.

Here is the circus ring.
It is a circle.
How many other round shapes
can you see?

The trapeze is swinging from side to side.
Show how it moves.
What pattern does the smoke make?
What other patterns can you see?

Look at the acrobats in line.
Which line has the tallest one first?
Find the two lines where he is last.
Are these lines both the same?

What shape have the acrobats made?
How many acrobats are in each row?
Who is at the top?

Here are some sets of animals.
Count the lions and the tigers.
Now count the tigers and the lions.

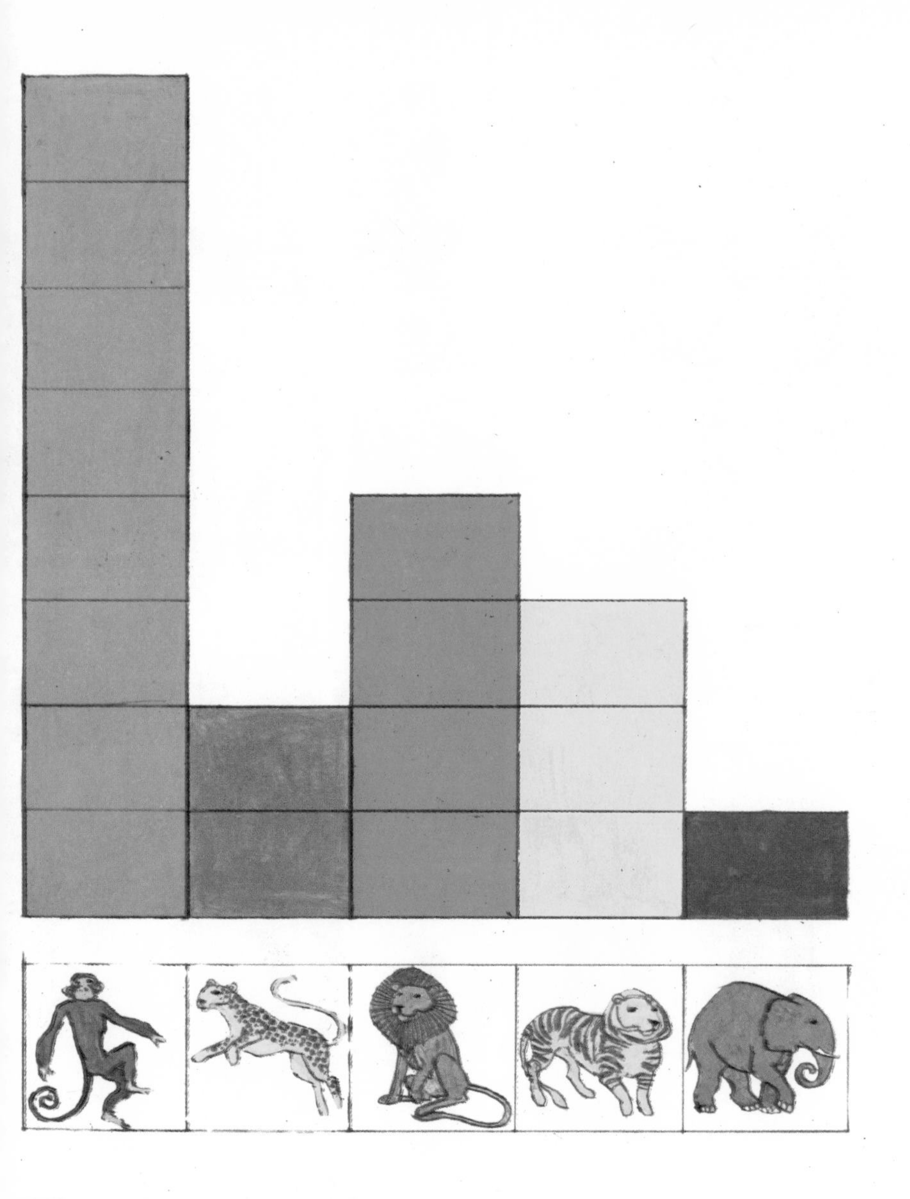

This is a graph
about the number of animals.
How many leopards are there?
Which set has the most animals?

The band plays a tune.
How many people are playing violins?
Are they all men?
How many are blowing instruments?

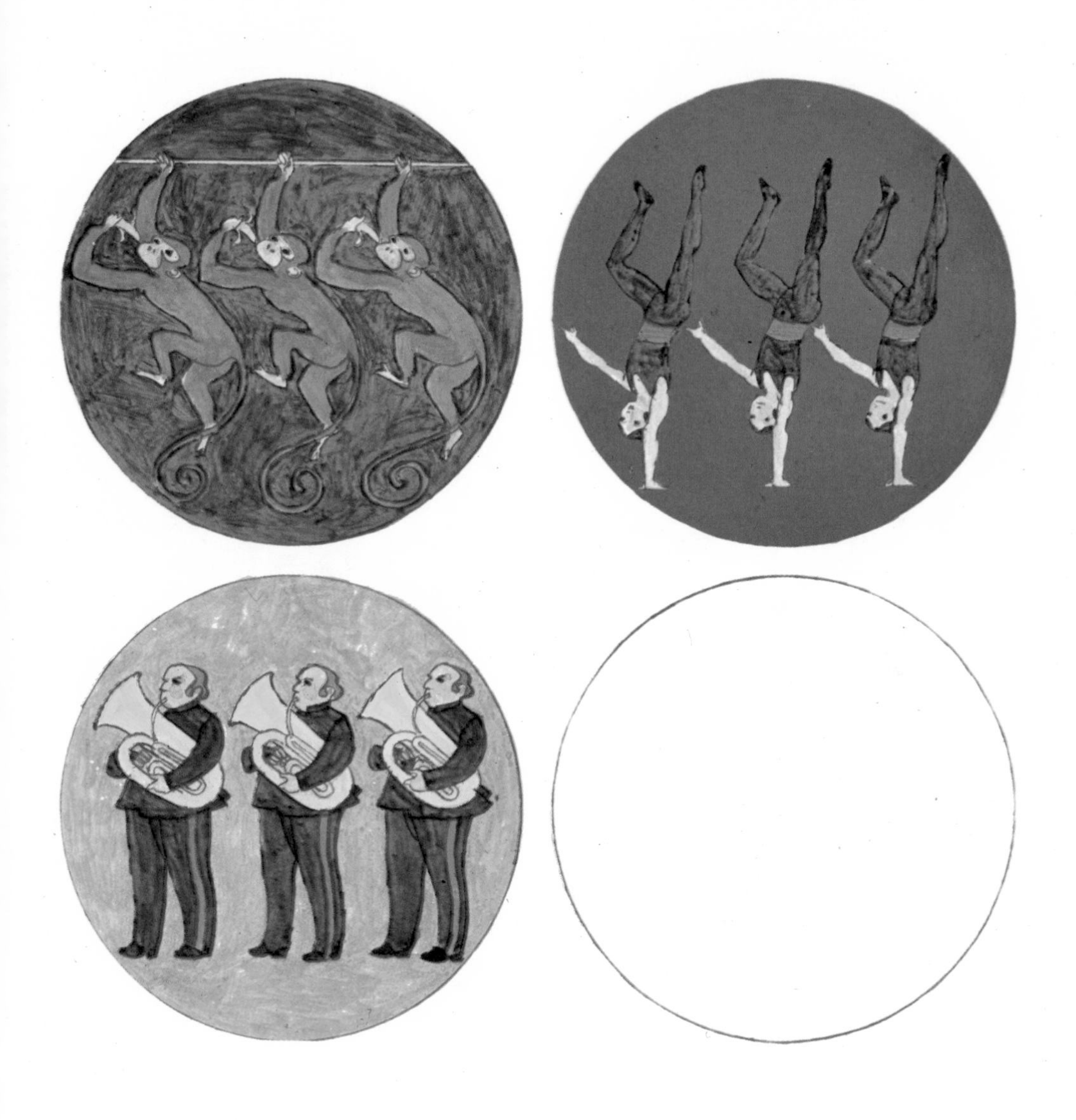

What is inside each circle?
How many are inside each circle?
What could you put in the empty circle?
How many would you put in it?

How many rungs has each ladder?
Which rung is the man on?
The lady is climbing to the top.
How many more rungs must she climb?

Which lady is the highest?
Is she higher than the man?
Which is the longest rope?
Is it longer than the net?

The strong man can lift one
hundred pounds.
The clown throws a bucket full of water.
How many quarts of water fill
your bucket?

Everything takes up space.
The elephant is not in any of the cages.
Why not?
Which animal takes up the least space?

One elephant stands on one tub.
How many people sit in one seat?
How many seats do 4 people need?

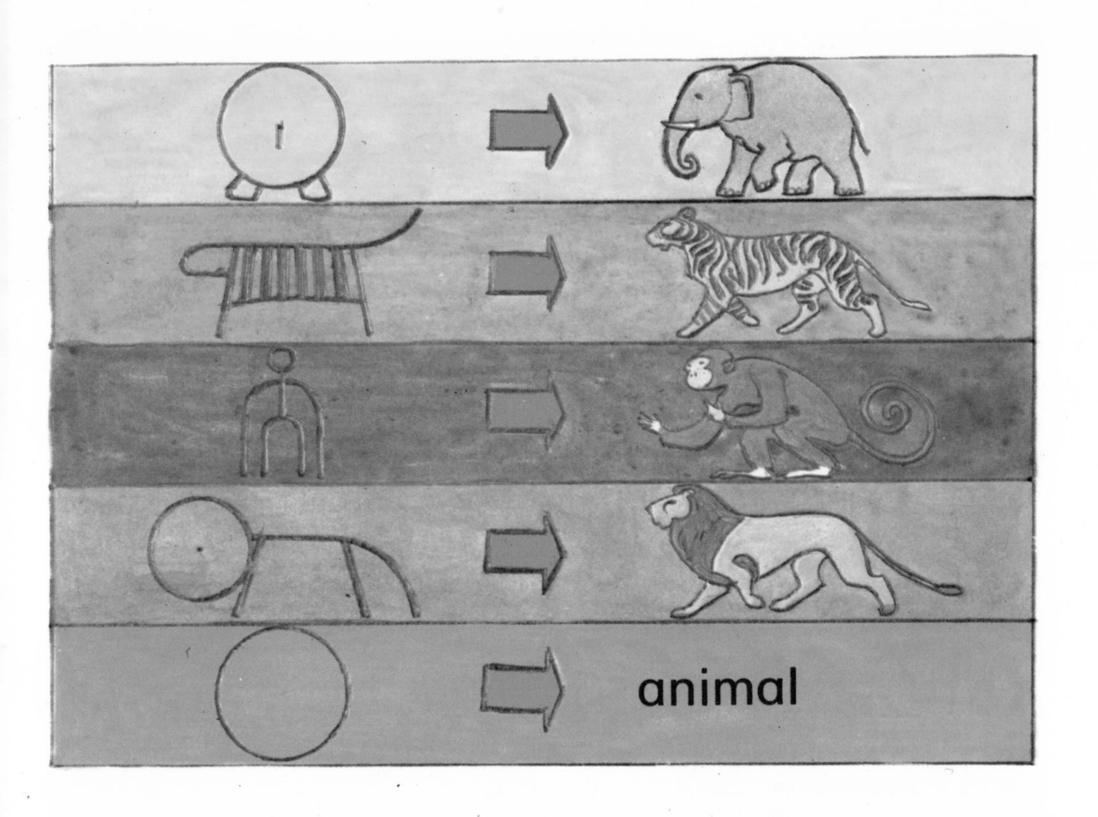

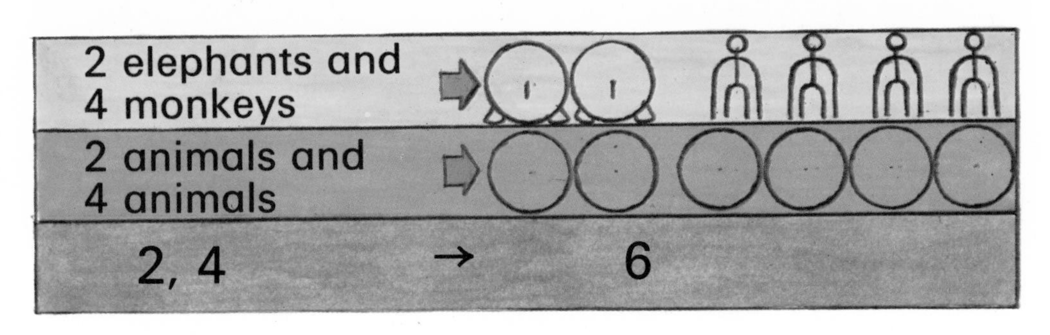

Can you make up some more like this?

The man covers the billboard
with the poster.
What are the clowns covering?
How many books will cover your table?

What is the clown doing?
What will happen to the face
on his balloon?

All kinds of patterns are being made.
Can you make patterns with your body?
Can you spin like the ball
and roll like the drum?

When you open the lid
the jack-in-the-box jumps up.
The spring inside pushes him.
Who else is pushed in the air?

Index

balancing
(page 8)

symmetry
(page 9)

circle
(page 10)

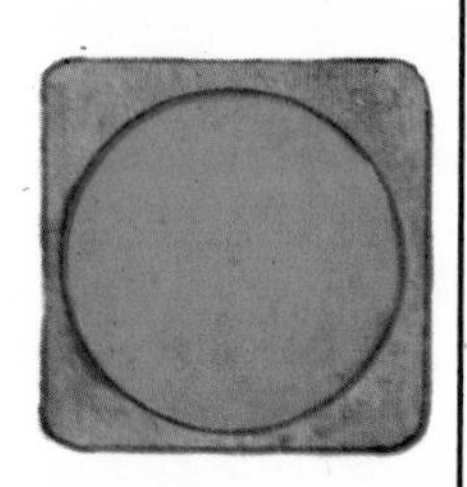

trapeze
(page 11)

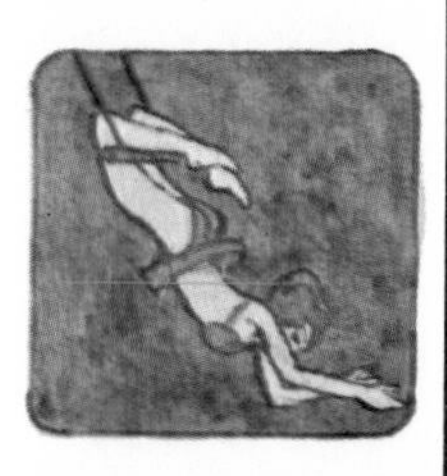

pattern
(page 11)

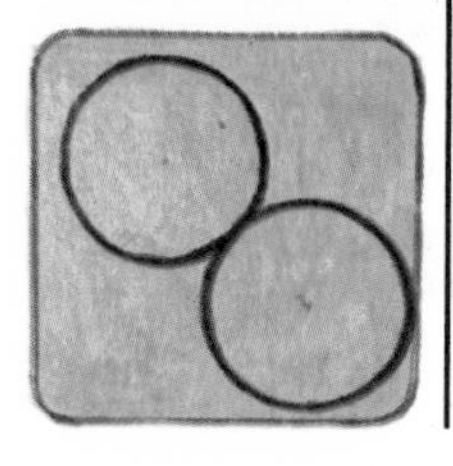

graph
(page 15)

instruments
(page 16)

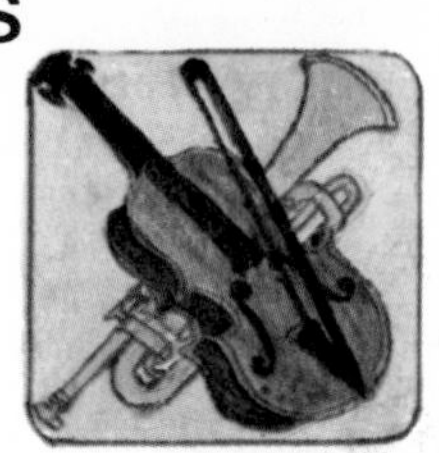

rung
(page 18)

pound
(page 20)

spring
(page 27)

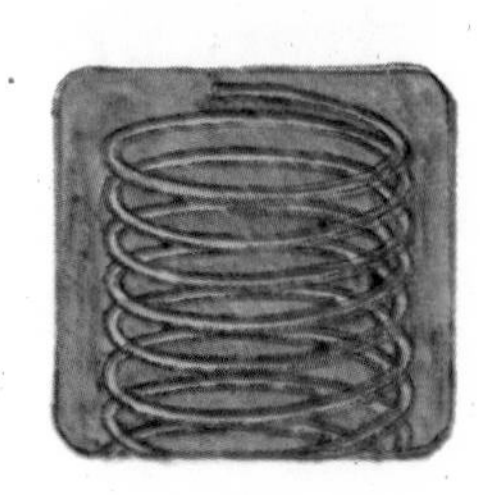